WILD WORK

BEAR

...OOPS ... POO?
A ZOO

Margie Markarian

Raintree

www.raintreepublishers.co.uk
Visit our website to find out
more information about
Raintree books.

To order:

☎ Phone 0845 6044371

🗎 Fax +44 (0) 1865 312263

✉ Email myorders@raintreepublishers.co.uk

Customers from outside the UK please telephone +44 1865 312262

Raintree is an imprint of Capstone Global Library Limited,
a company incorporated in England and Wales having its
registered office at 7 Pilgrim Street, London, EC4V 6LB –
Registered company number: 6695582

Edited by David Andrews, Nancy Dickmann, and Rebecca
Rissman
Designed by Victoria Allen
Picture research by Liz Alexander
Leveled by Marla Conn, with Read-Ability.
Originated by Dot Gradations Ltd
Printed and bound in China by Leo Paper Products

ISBN 978 1 4062 1677 6 (hardback)
15 14 13 12 11
10 9 8 7 6 5 4 3 2 1

ISBN 978 1 4062 1949 4 (paperback)
16 15 14 13 12
10 9 8 7 6 5 4 3 2 1

British Library Cataloguing in Publication Data
Markarian, Margie.
   Who scoops elephant poo? : working at a zoo. -- (Wild work)
   1. Zoos--Employees--Juvenile literature.
   I. Title II. Series
   636'.0889-dc22

Acknowledgements
The author and publisher are grateful to the following for
permission to reproduce copyright material: © Capstone
Publishers p. **11** (Karon Dubke); © Minnesota Zoo p. **8**;
Alamy pp. **4** (© Olaf Doering), **15** (© blickwinkel), **16** (© C.O.
Mercial), **20** (© Dave and Sigrun Tollerton), **23** (© Steven
May), **26** (© Bill Bachman), **27** (© Jeff Greenberg), **28** (©
Kuttig - RF – Kids); Corbis pp. **7** (© Nicky Loh/Reuters), **17**
(© Federico Gambarini), **19** (© Pavel Wolberg/epa); Getty
Images pp. **12** (Peter Macdiarmid), **14** (William West/AFP),
18 (Jessie Cohen/Smithsonian National Zoo), **21** (WireImage),
22 (Christopher Hunt), **29** (Thinkstock); Photolibrary pp. **5**
(Jochen Tack/imagebroker.net), **13** (Jochen Tack/imagebroker.
net), **24** (Michael DeYoung/Alaskastock), **25** (TAO Images
Limited); Rex Features p. **6** (Andrew Price); Shutterstock
pp. **9** (© G. Campbell), **10** (© ivylingpy).

Background design features reproduced with permission of
Shutterstock (© Vard). Cover photograph reproduced with
permission of Shutterstock (© Galyna Andrushko).

Every effort has been made to contact copyright holders
of material reproduced in this book. Any omissions will
be rectified in subsequent printings if notice is given to
the publisher.

All the Internet addresses (URLs) given in this book were valid
at the time of going to press. However, due to the dynamic
nature of the Internet, some addresses may have changed, or
sites may have changed or ceased to exist since publication.
While the author and publisher regret any inconvenience this
may cause readers, no responsibility for any such changes can
be accepted by either the author or the publisher.

Contents

Wild about animals

People who work in zoos are wild about animals. They hang out with monkeys. They get cosy with giraffes. Sometimes they swim with sharks. But that's not all they do!

DID YOU KNOW?

The world's first public zoo was set up around 1470 B.C. in Ancient Egypt.

Collecting creatures

It takes a team of people to run a zoo. Head **curators** (say *cue-RAY-tors*) lead the team. They decide which animals will live in the zoo.

Some zoos let you see animals up close.

They make rules about animal care, train the other zoo workers, and help design **exhibits**.

Building home sweet home

Habitat designers create living spaces for zoo animals. They try to copy the animal's natural habitat. This helps keep the animals happy and healthy.

Habitat designers have given this bear rocks and logs to climb on, and water to splash in.

The green team

Pandas eat bamboo. Giraffes chomp on leaves. Zebras chew on grass. **Horticulturists** (say *HOR-tih-CUL-chur-ists*) are plant scientists. They make sure zoo animals have the trees, bushes, grasses, and other plants they need.

Horticulturists create areas that look good and are full of the right things to eat!

Who feeds the llamas lunch?

Zookeepers take care of the animals. They make their meals and set out the food. They keep track of how much the animals eat.

Zookeepers check on the animals every morning and make sure they are safe at night. They understand and respect animals.

Who scoops elephant poo?

Cleaning up after animals is a stinky job, but zookeepers don't mind. They hose down hippos. They brush sea lion teeth! They even scoop elephant poo!

sea lion

DID YOU KNOW?

Elephant poo can be **recycled** and made into paper products.

15

Open up and say Aaah!

What happens when a gorilla has stomach ache or a leopard cuts its paw? The zoo's medical team comes to the rescue!

Veterinarians are zoo doctors. They take care of animals when they are ill, hurt, or having babies.

When an animal needs an **operation** or gives birth, **veterinary technicians** help the veterinarian. They comfort the animal.

Veterinary technicians also give injections, wrap broken bones, and take temperatures. Sometimes they even give the animals x-rays!

Who cuddles the koalas?

At many zoos visitors can handle some of the smaller animals. An animal handler leads these sessions. They understand what the animals need and how they behave.

DID YOU KNOW?

Many animal handlers started by training their pets or farm animals.

What's the buzz?

Insects are part of the animal world, too. **Entomologists** (say *EN-tome-OL-oh-jists*) create zoo **exhibits** starring chirping crickets and beautiful butterflies. They are scientists who study insects. Spider experts show visitors hairy tarantulas.

DID YOU KNOW?

Tarantulas don't usually bother humans. A tarantula bite is like a bee sting. It hurts, but it's not deadly unless you are **allergic** to it.

tarantula

Flipping for fins

Some zoos are home to sea creatures. **Aquarists** (say *a-KWA-rists*) take care of fish and other sea animals. They check the tank water and make sure it's the right temperature. They dive in to clean the tanks. They care for plants and even feed hungry sharks!

Teaching others

Zoo education officers share their love and knowledge of animals with visitors. They lead tours and give visitors information about the animals. They enjoy being with animals and talking to people.

Could you work at a zoo?

If you love working with all types of animals, you could have a zoo career. But the jobs are hard to get!

It helps to study animal science. You should get experience working with animals. Caring for pets or farm animals, or working at an animal shelter, can help you get a job at a zoo.

Glossary

allergic being sensitive to some plants, animals, or materials. Allergies can make some people ill.

aquarist a person who cares for fish and other sea creatures

curator a person who takes care of animal exhibits at a zoo or objects in collections at museums

endangered species type of animal in danger of dying out

entomologist a scientist who studies insects and spiders

exhibits displays at zoos or museums

habitat the natural home of an animal

horticulturist a scientist who studies plants

operation something done inside the body to help humans and other animals. Doctors and veterinatians do operations.

recycle use again in another form

veterinarian a doctor who takes care of animals

veterinary technician a person who assists a veterinarian (vet)

Find out more

Books to read

New Zoos, Bob Barton (Longman, 2004)

Wild Animals (1000 Things You Should Know), John Farndon (Miles Kelly, 2005)

Wow! Animal (Dorling Kindersley, 2009)

Websites to visit

http://www.zsl.org/

The Zoological Society of London's website has information about London and Whipsnade Zoos and tells you more about different careers in zoos.

http://kids.nationalgeographic.com/Animals

Fun facts and photos about dozens of amazing wild animals and their habitats.

http://animal.discovery.com/guides/endangered/endangered.html

From giant armadillos to snow leopards, learn about some of the world's most endangered species.

Index

Freddie goes to the seaside

Nicola Smee

little ORCHARD

Please return/renew this item
by the last date shown.
Books may also be renewed by
phone and Internet

ORCHARD BOOKS
338 Euston Road, London NW1 3BH
Orchard Books Australia
Level 17/207 Kent Street, Sydney, NSW 2000
First published in 1999 by Orchard Books
This edition published in 2003
978 1 84362 216 1
Copyright © Nicola Smee 1999
The right of Nicola Smee to be identified as
the author and illustrator of this work has been asserted by her
in accordance with the Copyright, Design and Patents Act, 1988.
A CIP catalogue record for this book is available from the British Library.
1 3 5 7 9 10 8 6 4 2
Printed in China
Orchard Books is a division of Hachette Children's Books,
an Hachette Livre UK company.

Mum's taking me and Bear
to the seaside! Hurray!

I can see the sea!
Bear can see the sea!
But I saw it first!

The sun is so hot Mum says
we must put on sun cream
and sunhats so we don't burn.

I show Bear how to
make sandcastles.
(I learnt at playschool.)
You need water to make
the sand stick!

We left the crab in the rock pool, but we're taking some seashells home to make a shell necklace for Mum.